Written by E. Amber Finch
Created & Designed by E. Amber Finch
Edited by Jazmine Keeton

The Adventures of Peeps:
Peeps Goes to Panama is dedicated to
Grandma Carol Finch.

We love and miss you so much. Thank
you for being a fabulous inspiration.
Without you, there would be no Peeps!

Peeps loved her home at the cafe. She has lived at the cafe for 5 years.

The owner's of the cafe are retiring and the cafe is going to close.

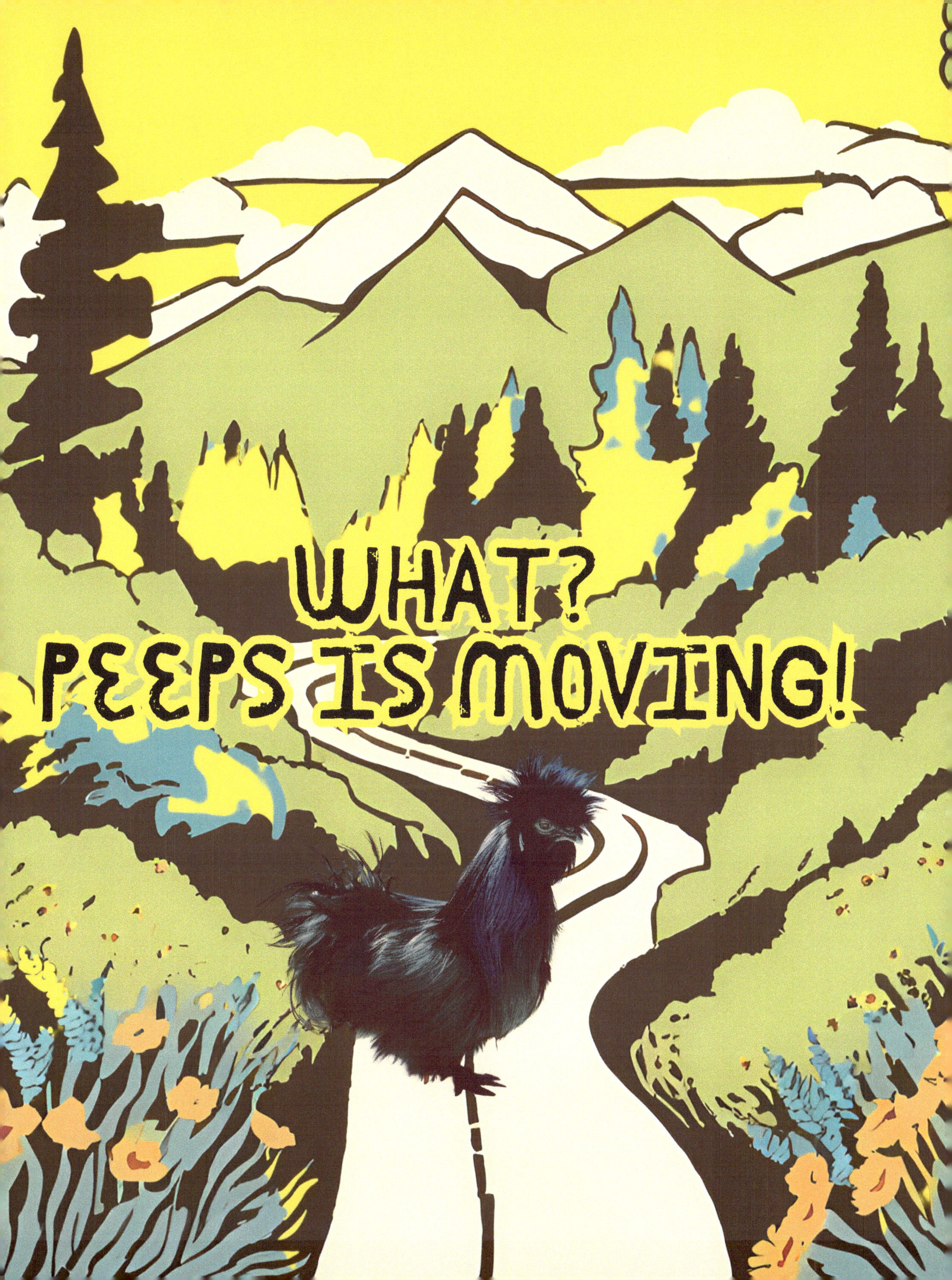
WHAT?
PEEPS IS MOVING!

Peeps sat by the window in the camper, excited for this new adventure!

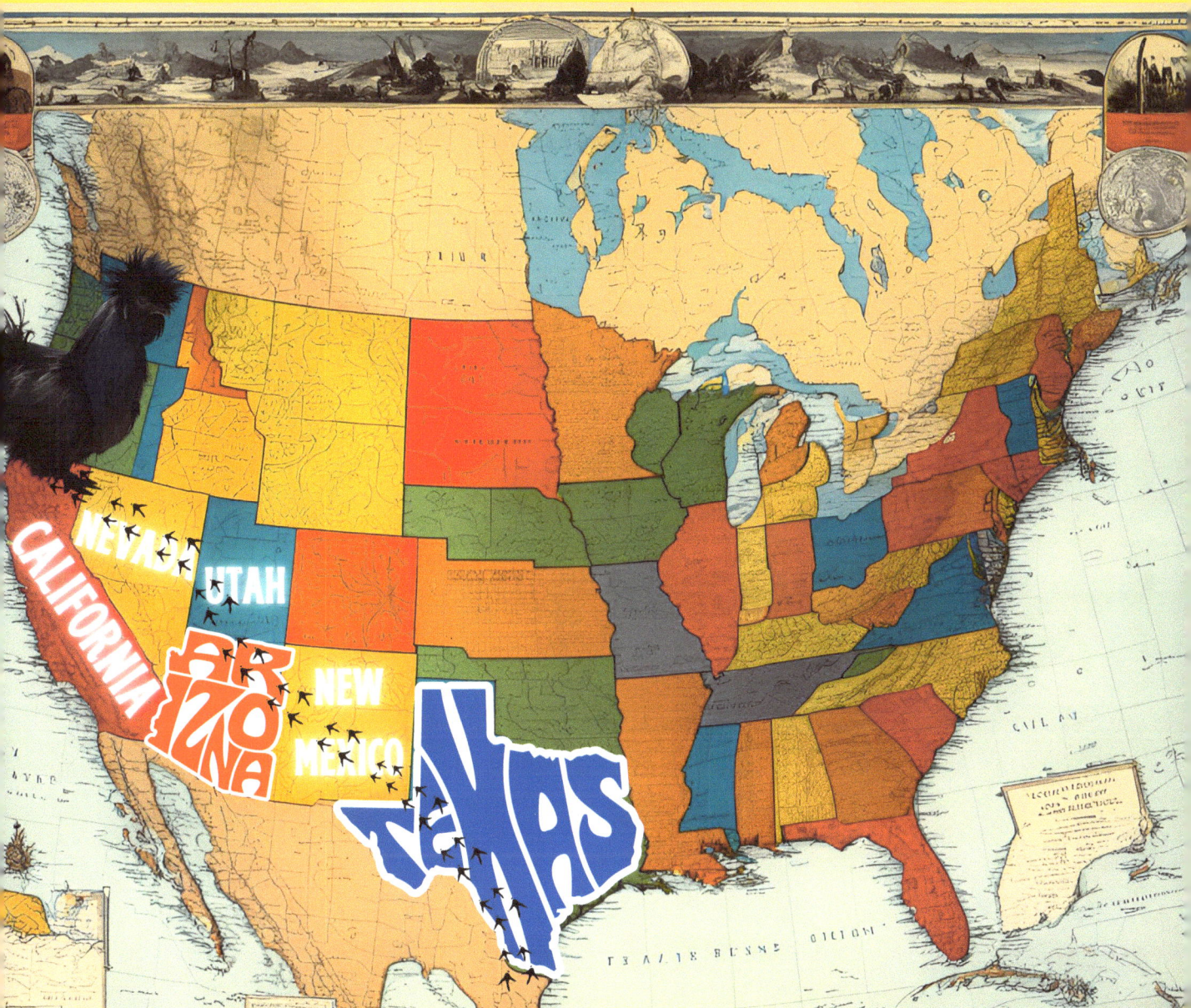

CALIFORNIA

NEVADA

UTAH

ARIZONA

NEW MEXICO

TEXAS

Peeps traveled through six states to get to the Mexico border!

Peeps needed a passport to enter Central America! Oh no, she did not have one! Peeps had to be very quiet traveling across the Mexican border! You may say "She had to sneak into the country."

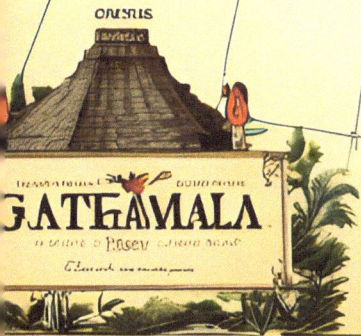

Peeps weaved a shawl in Guatemala.
She enjoyed seeing the ancient Mayan carvings.

Peeps met a seagull along the way. Seagulls love flying down the coast and stealing snacks from beach-goers!

"Hi Peeps, my name is Scarlett!"

Peeps tells Scarlett, “it’s snack time. What’s your favorite snack?”

Peeps learned that Scarlett’s favorite snack is pickles!

Peeps tried baleadas in Honduras! Baleadas is a type of taco.

Peeps says "The tres leches in Nicaragua is delicious!"

The flatbread known as pupusas in El Salvador filled Peeps up!

On Peeps' adventure through Central America she saw rare animals.

Sloth

Viper Snake

Tortoise

Jaguar

Peeps stopped at the Costa Rican beach to see the big waves. She had a blast surfing!

Costa Rica

Finally, Peeps' journey across country ends: Panama is Peeps' new home!

Peeps traveled 4,380 miles to get to Panama. She is excited to share her adventures in Panama with you.

PANAMA

Learn with Peeps:

1) What state did Peeps live in before she traveled to Panama?

Peeps lived in California.

2) How many states did Peeps travel through to get to the Mexico border?

Peeps traveled through six states.

3) What was Scarlett's favorite snack?

Scarlett loves pickles.

4) What animal was your favorite that Peeps saw in Central America?

Peeps saw a jaguar, sloth, tortoise, and viper snake.

Peeps favorite animal is the sloth.

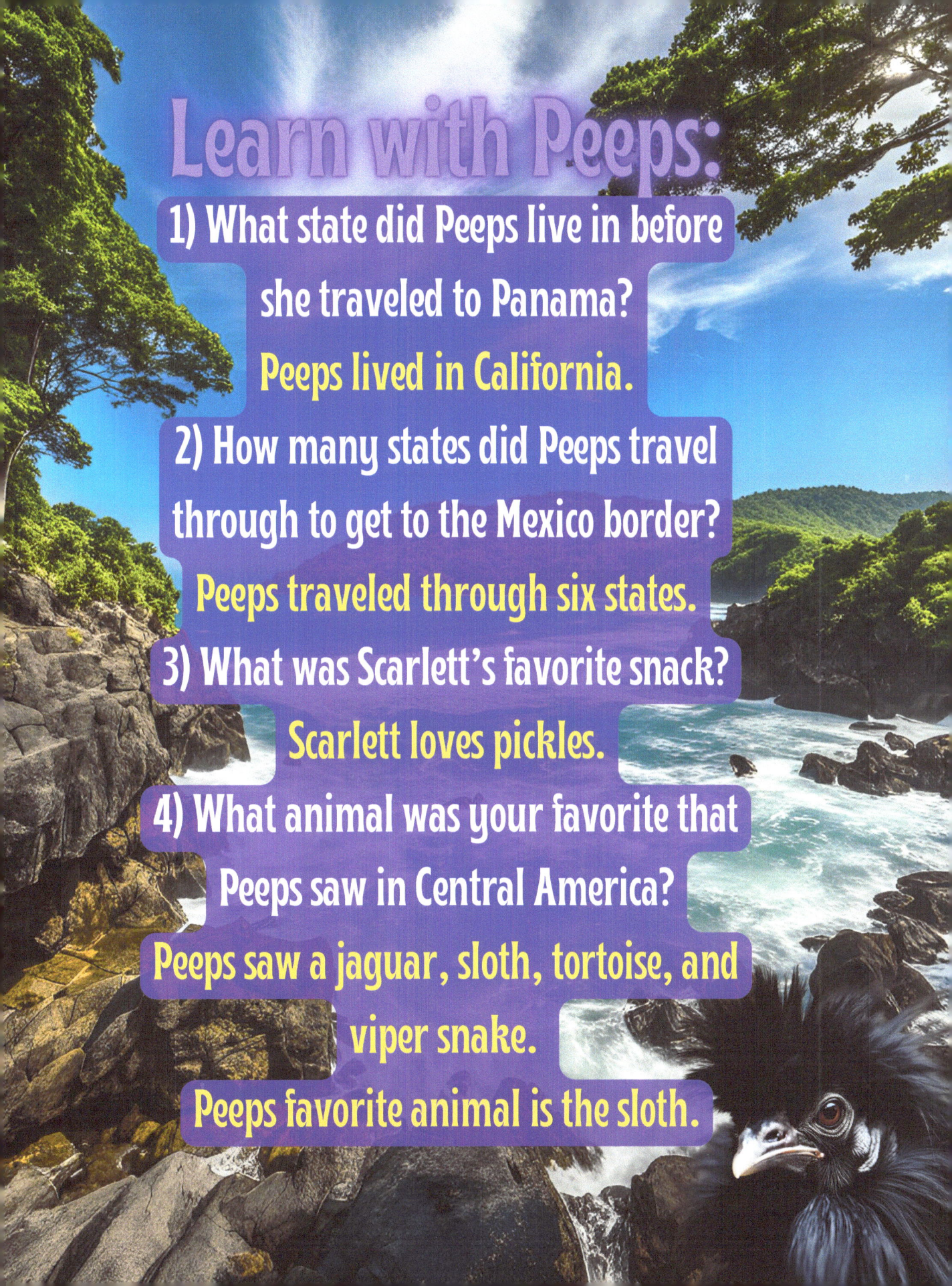

ABOUT ME

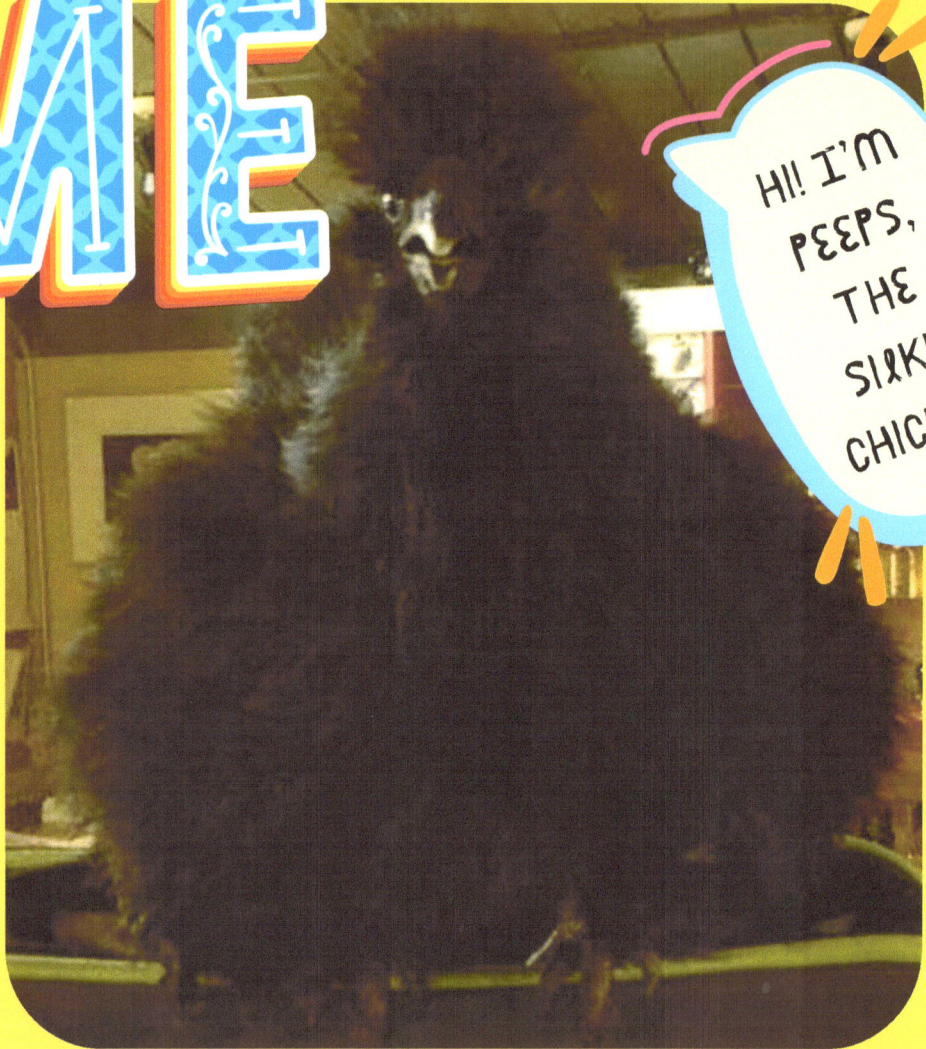

HI! I'M PEEPS, THE SILKIE CHICKEN!

Peeps is a REAL chicken who did live in a cafe in California and traveled to Panama.

Thank you for reading The Adventure of Peeps: Peeps Goes to Panama written by E. Amber Finch.

Look forward to more adventures with Peeps.

Peeps Learns About Panama

Peeps Learns How to Farm

Peeps Goes to Market

www.ingramcontent.com/pod-product-compliance
Lightning Source LLC
Chambersburg PA
CBHW060807090426
42736CB00002B/183